D0754698

What's in Your Fast Food?

WHAT'S IN YOUR PIZZA?

Jaclyn Sullivan

PowerKiDS press™

New York

To Miranda and the summer of pizza

Published in 2012 by The Rosen Publishing Group, Inc.
29 East 21st Street, New York, NY 10010

First Edition

Editor: Sara Antill
Book Design: Greg Tucker

Photo Credits: Cover, pp. 5, 8, 14, 15, 22 Shutterstock.com; pp. 4, 18–19 Jupiterimages/Brand X Pictures/Thinkstock; pp. 6, 10, 12 iStockphoto/Thinkstock; p. 7 (top) Eric Vandeville/Gamma-Rapho via Getty Images; p. 7 (bottom) Taesam Do/Getty Images; pp. 9, 11 (left), 16, 17 (left) Hemera/Thinkstock; p. 11 (top) Stockbyte/Thinkstock; p. 13 Jupiterimages/Photos.com/Thinkstock; pp. 17 (top), 21 Jupiterimages/Comstock/Thinkstock; p. 18 (left) Comstock/Thinkstock; p. 20 Jupiterimages/Goodshoot/Thinkstock.

Library of Congress Cataloging-in-Publication Data

Sullivan, Jaclyn.
 What's in your pizza? / by Jaclyn Sullivan. — 1st ed.
    p. cm. — (What's in your fast food)
 Includes index.
 ISBN 978-1-4488-6209-2 (library binding) — ISBN 978-1-4488-6377-8 (pbk.) —
 ISBN 978-1-4488-6378-5 (6-pack)
 1. Pizza—Juvenile literature. 2. Convenience foods—Juvenile literature. I. Title.
 TX770.P58S85 2012
 641.82'48—dc23
                                   2011030805

Manufactured in the United States of America

CPSIA Compliance Information: Batch #WW12PK: For Further Information contact Rosen Publishing, New York, New York at 1-800-237-9932

Contents

Popular Pizza

This boy is playing basketball. The more active we are, the more energy our bodies need.

Have you ever had a slice of hot, cheesy pizza? Pizza is often eaten at sports games and parties. It can be eaten for either lunch or dinner. Some people even eat pizza for breakfast! Most Americans eat pizza at least once a month.

Like all food, pizza gives our bodies **energy**. Energy is what allows our bodies to grow, move, think, and breathe. We need the energy from food to survive. Some

Pizza is a popular food to serve at parties because it is easy to share. One or two pizzas are usually enough to feed several people.

foods are better for us than others, though. Have you ever wondered if pizza was a healthy choice? Learning about what is in pizza can help you decide!

From Italy to America

Pizza as we know it came from Naples, Italy. In 1889, a baker named Rafaele Esposito was asked to make a pizza for Queen Margherita of Italy. He put tomatoes, basil, and mozzarella, a kind of cheese, on the pizza. Esposito's pizza was so popular that it became the model for modern pizzas.

Green, white, and red are the colors of the Italian flag, seen here. Esposito wanted the green basil, white mozzarella, and red tomatoes on his pizza to look like the Italian flag.

Pizza came to America when large groups of Italians **immigrated**, or moved, to the United States. In 1905, an Italian immigrant opened America's first pizza restaurant in New York City. It took some time for pizza to become popular. By the 1950s, though, many Americans were eating pizza.

Margherita was the queen of Italy from 1878 until 1900. Today, a pizza with a thin crust, tomatoes, basil, and mozzarella is often called a pizza Margherita.

FAST-FOOD FACTS

People around the world enjoy many kinds of pizza toppings. In Brazil, some people like green peas on their pizza. In Japan, eel and squid are popular toppings!

7

Pizza Dough

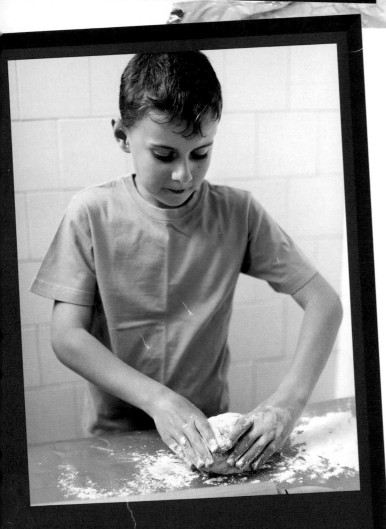

This boy is shaping a ball of dough. The white flour on his hands and the table keeps the dough from sticking.

Pizza **dough** makes the crust, or base, of a pizza. Pizza dough is made from flour, water, salt, and yeast. Flour is a fine powder made from a grain called wheat. It is used to make most types of bread.

Yeast is a living thing that helps baked foods rise, or puff up. Foods that are baked without yeast, like crackers, do not rise. Yeast eats the sugars in food for energy. When yeast eats the

This man is tossing pizza dough into the air to make it very thin and round. Tossing pizza dough like this takes a lot of practice.

natural sugars in flour, this creates bubbles of a gas called **carbon dioxide**. The bubbles make the dough rise. The dough can then be stretched and baked into a pizza crust.

Turning Tomatoes into Sauce

Most pizzas are topped with tomato sauce. Many people think tomatoes are a vegetable. However, tomatoes are actually a fruit! Tomatoes grow on vines. Florida grows the most tomatoes in the United States every year.

To make tomato sauce, tomatoes are squashed and cooked with salt, sugar, garlic, and **seasonings** such as basil and oregano. Sometimes tomato sauce is made from

Tomatoes originally grew only in Central America and South America. They were brought to Europe by Spanish explorers in the sixteenth century.

FAST-FOOD FACTS

More than one billion pizzas are delivered in the United States every year! More pizzas are delivered on Super Bowl Sunday than on any other day of the year.

tomato paste instead of whole tomatoes. Tomato paste is made by cooking tomatoes for many hours. A little bit of paste goes a long way in a sauce. The sauce on many frozen and delivery pizzas is made with tomato paste.

Tomato sauce is usually spread on the pizza dough before it is baked. This woman is using a spoon to spread the sauce.

Cheese, Please!

One type of mozzarella, found mostly in Italy, is made from the milk of a water buffalo, seen here. Most mozzarella in the United States is made from cow's milk, though.

Look at any pizza and it will most likely be topped with some kind of cheese! Cheese is made from milk. Most milk for cheese comes from cows. Other cheeses are made from the milk of animals like goats and sheep. There are hundreds of types of cheeses, and they are made in different ways. Some, such as Brie, are soft. Others, such as Romano, are hard cheeses.

Many pizzas are topped with a mix of several cheeses. Different cheeses add different flavors to pizza.

Mozzarella is often used on pizza. This is because it is soft and melts well. Sometimes other cheeses, like provolone, Parmesan, and feta are used on pizza as well.

Frozen pizzas are very popular because they come in different sizes and they can be cooked very quickly.

Have you ever eaten frozen pizza? Frozen pizzas can be bought at the store and baked at home. Frozen pizzas are often made in factories. In these factories, pizza crusts are baked in giant ovens. The crusts go through machines that drop tomato sauce and cheese on them. Another machine drops toppings, like pepperoni, onto the pizzas. The pizzas are then frozen in giant freezers and wrapped in plastic. One factory can make thousands of pizzas in a day!

Frozen pizzas can last for a long time. Some frozen pizzas can be kept in the freezer for up to one year without going bad!

Frozen pizzas are often kept in the frozen-foods aisle of the grocery store. They need to be kept frozen until it is time for them to be cooked.

Pizza Processing

Fresh vegetables, like these, are often called whole foods. This is because they have not been cooked or processed in any way. These foods still have all of their natural nutrients.

Have you ever wondered how frozen pizzas can keep for so long? It is because they have **preservatives** in them. Preservatives make food last longer. Frozen pizzas also often have dyes called **artificial** colors. The dyes keep the colors in frozen pizzas looking fresh.

Some of the foods we eat are in their natural form. Many foods,

FAST-FOOD FACTS

Pepperoni is made from ground pork and beef. Sugar, salt, spices, and preservatives are also added. It is then dried so that it can be eaten.

though, are **processed**, or changed from their natural form. Generally, the more a food has been processed, the more of its **nutrients** it loses. We need the nutrients from food so our bodies can stay healthy. The toppings on frozen pizzas have often been processed and have few nutrients in them.

Frozen and delivery pizzas sometimes have artificial flavors added to them. These man-made flavors replace flavors that were lost during processing.

Fat and Calories

The amount of energy a food gives us is measured in **calories**. Most kids need between 1,600 and 1,800 calories a day. Eating the right number of calories each day keeps you healthy. However, if you do not use all the calories that you eat, your body stores those extra calories as fat.

Some parts of a pizza, such as cheese and pepperoni, have a lot of calories. Pizza does not have to be an unhealthy food, though. Cheese has calcium, a nutrient that makes our bones strong. Tomato sauce and fresh vegetable toppings have **vitamins** that help our brains, muscles, and blood stay healthy.

This girl is adding cheese to her homemade pizza. When you make a pizza yourself, you can control how much of each topping you use.

These kids have gathered vegetables from a garden. Starting a garden in your backyard is a great way to get fresh vegetables without spending a lot of money at the grocery store.

Nutrition Facts

How do you know if a food is good for you? Check the label to learn more about your pizza! The label on a box of frozen pizza will list all the **ingredients** in the pizza. The label will also show you the amounts of calories and fat in the pizza, as well as the amounts of vitamins and nutrients.

Many companies list nutritional facts for their food products on their Web sites. If the nutritional facts are not listed, you can call the company and ask for the information.

This label shows the nutritional facts for one slice of cheese pizza. You can use math to figure out the amounts for two slices or the whole pizza.

Nutrition Facts

Serving Size 1 slice (90g)
Servings Per Container: 8

Amount Per Serving

Calories 250   Calories from Fat 110

	% Daily Value *
Total Fat 13g	19%
Saturated Fat 6g	29%
Trans Fat 0g	
Cholesterol 25mg	8%
Sodium 690mg	29%
Total Carbohydrate 37g	12%
Dietary Fiber 2g	6%
Sugar 3g	
Protein 16g	32%

Vitamin A 8%	•	Vitamin C 0%
Calcium 25%	•	Iron 15%

*Percent Daily Values are based on a 2,000 calorie diet. Your daily values may be higher or lower depending on your calorie needs.

	Calories	2,000	2,500
Total Fat	Less than	65g	80g
Sat Fat	Less than	20g	25g
Cholesterol	Less than	300mg	300mg
Sodium	Less than	300mg	300mg
Total Carbohydrate		300g	375g
Dietary Fiber		25g	30g

Calories per gram:
Fat 9   •   Carbohydrate 4   •   Protein 4

To find nutrition facts for pizza at a restaurant, try checking the restaurant's Web site. You can ask cafeteria workers at your school to tell you about the nutrition of the pizza they serve there. Knowing the facts about nutrition can help you make good choices.

FAST-FOOD FACTS

The calories and nutritional facts listed on labels are for one serving of pizza. One serving of pizza is generally one or two slices, not a whole pizza!

Healthy Pizza

It is important to make healthy choices about the foods you eat. If you make homemade pizza, try using fresh toppings, such as tomatoes, peppers, or mushrooms. These are often healthier than processed toppings like pepperoni or sausage. This is because they have more nutrients and less fat.

Asking for less cheese on your pizza will also help you eat less fat and fewer calories. Fruit and vegetable toppings are low in calories, too. Homemade pizza can be healthy and very tasty!

These girls are topping their pizza with broccoli and other fresh vegetables. Vegetable toppings are a healthy choice for pizza.

Glossary

artificial (ar-tih-FIH-shul) Made by people, not nature.

calories (KA-luh-reez) Amounts of food that the body uses to keep working.

carbon dioxide (KAHR-bun dy-OK-syd) An odorless, colorless gas. People breathe out carbon dioxide.

dough (DOH) A thick mix from which food is made.

energy (EH-ner-jee) The power to work or to act.

immigrated (IH-muh-grayt-ed) Moved to another country to live.

ingredients (in-GREE-dee-unts) The different things that go into food.

nutrients (NOO-tree-ents) Food that a living thing needs to live and grow.

preservatives (prih-ZER-vuh-tivz) Substances that keep something from going bad.

processed (PRAH-sesd) Changed by a set of actions.

seasonings (SEEZ-ningz) Ingredients, such as herbs and spices, that add flavor to food.

vitamins (VY-tuh-minz) Nutrients to help the body fight illness and grow strong.

Index

Web Sites

Due to the changing nature of Internet links, PowerKids Press has developed an online list of Web sites related to the subject of this book. This site is updated regularly. Please use this link to access the list:

www.powerkidslinks.com/food/pizza/